Biblical Fou

Called to Minister

by Larry Kreider

House To House Publications
Lititz, Pennsylvania USA

Called to Minister

Larry Kreider

Updated Edition © 2002, Reprinted 2003, 2006
Copyright © 1993, 1997, 1999
House to House Publications
11 Toll Gate Road, Lititz, PA 17543
Telephone: 800.848.5892
Web site: www.dcfi.org

ISBN 1-886973-10-5
Design and illustrations by Sarah Sauder

CONTENTS

Books in this Series

This is the eleventh book in a twelve-book series designed to help believers to build a solid biblical foundation in their lives.

A corresponding *Biblical Foundations for Children* book is also available (see page 63).

Introduction

The foundation of the Christian faith is built on Jesus Christ and His Word to us, the Holy Bible. This twelve-book *Biblical Foundation Series* includes elementary principles every Christian needs to help lay a strong spiritual foundation in his or her life.

In this eleventh Biblical Foundation book, *Called to Minister,* we discover that every Christian is called by God to minister to other people. The Lord has called pastors and other spiritual leaders to train the saints so that every believer can be involved in ministry and become mature in Christ. As each believer fulfills what the Lord has called him to do, a wonderful thing happens. God begins to build His church through His people from house to house and in each community. Ministry does not just happen in our church meetings; it happens at our schools, our places of work, and in our homes as we reach out to others.

In this book, the foundation truths from the Word of God are presented with modern day parables that help you easily understand the basics of Christianity. Use this book and the other 11 *Biblical Foundation* books to lay a solid spiritual foundation in your life, or if you are already a mature Christian, these books are great tools to assist you in discipling others. May His Word become life to you today.

God bless you!

Larry Kreider

How to Use This Resource

Personal study

Read from start to finish as an individual study program to build a firm Christian foundation and develop spiritual maturity.

- Each chapter has a key verse excellent to commit to memory.
- Additional scriptures in gray boxes are used for further study.
- Each reading includes questions for personal reflection and room to journal at the end of the book.

Daily devotional

Use as a devotional for a daily study of God's Word.

- Each chapter is divided into 7-day sections for weekly use.
- Additional days at the end of the book bring the total number of devotionals to one complete month. The complete set of 12 books gives one year's worth of daily devotionals.
- Additional scriptures are used for further study.
- Each day includes reflection questions and a place to write answers at the end of the book.

Mentoring relationship

Use for a spiritual parenting relationship to study, pray and discuss life applications together.

- A spiritual father or mother can easily take a spiritual son or daughter through these short Bible study lessons and use the reflection questions to provoke dialogue about what is learned.
- Read each day or an entire chapter at a time.

Small group study

Study this important biblical foundation in a small group setting.

- The teacher studies the material in the chapters and teaches, using the user-friendly outline provided at the end of the book.

Taught as a biblical foundation course

These teachings can be taught by a pastor or other Christian leader as a basic Biblical foundation course.

- Students read an assigned portion of the material.
- In the class, the leader teaches the assigned material using the chapter outlines at the end of the book.

CHAPTER 1

Everyone Can Minister

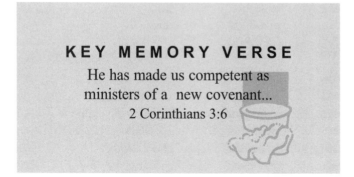

KEY MEMORY VERSE

He has made us competent as
ministers of a new covenant...
2 Corinthians 3:6

We are equipped to minister

Recently a soccer enthusiast told me of his experience at one of the World Cup soccer games. He paid $150 for a seat and joined thousands of fans who watched 22 talented players kick a ball around on a soccer field. Although he loved soccer, he was not allowed to play—he was a spectator only. His story reminded me of the church today. Think about it. A group of "spectator" Christians gathers together each Sunday morning to watch as the pastor performs his duties. Is this what the Lord desires for His church? I do not believe so. Every believer can be a minister.

Pastors or other church leaders are in place to help or equip every believer to minister. The Bible tells us in Ephesians 4:11-12 that the Lord releases spiritual leaders with specific gifts for two basic purposes: *And He Himself gave some to be apostles, some prophets, some evangelists, and some pastors and teachers, for the equipping of the saints for the work of ministry, for the edifying of the body of Christ (NKJ).*

According to this scripture, these spiritual leaders with particular gifts are given to "equip the saints to do the work of ministry" and to "build up (edify) the body of Christ." Christ gives these leaders specific leadership gifts so that they can prepare God's people for works of service and so the body of Christ can grow as God intended.

When these leaders train and equip every saint to minister, the church grows. If every believer does not learn how to serve others, God's church becomes paralyzed: only part of the body is being used.

REFLECTION

What is the role of spiritual leaders in the church, according to Ephesians 4:11-12? How do these leaders train us to minister?

If most of your body parts would shut down, you would be suffering from a partial paralysis. Much of the church of Jesus Christ today has become paralyzed because the important truth of all the saints doing the work of ministry is overlooked. God is restoring a basic truth to His church which involves the dynamic of every believer being called as a minister.

The leadership of the early church, including apostles, prophets, evangelists, pastors and teachers, realized that their focus needed to be on prayer and ministering the Word of God. *We will...give our attention to prayer and the ministry of the word (Acts 6:3b-4).*

Before they could "give themselves continually to prayer and the ministry of the Word," the leaders had to train each believer to minister, thus easing the burden of doing everything themselves. As they obeyed this spiritual principle, thousands came into the kingdom of God and the church grew rapidly during the first century.

Everyone can serve

Since the scriptures tell us that the saints are called to do the work of ministry, let's look again at who the saints really are. The truth is this: If you are a Christian, born again by the Spirit of God, you are a saint. We do not become saints when we get to heaven. We are saints right now. When you look in the mirror in the morning, I encourage you to say, "I am a saint." The Bible says the saints are the ones who are called to do the work of ministry (Ephesians 4:12). Thousands of believers today are unfulfilled because they are not fulfilling the purpose that God intended for them—to minister to others.

What does the word *ministry* or *minister* really mean? Webster's 1828 dictionary says, "to minister means to serve, to wait, or to attend." If you go to a restaurant, the waiter or waitress is ministering to you. They serve you or wait on you at your table. That is a type of ministry. If you go to a hospital, you will see hospital attendants who are waiting, serving or ministering to the patients. The term *serve* and *minister* can be used interchangeably.

Every Christian is called by God to minister to other people. It is a privilege to minister and to serve others in Jesus' name. There are many different ways to minister and many different types of ministry; however, each person is called to serve others in the name of Jesus. The Bible says in Mark 16:17-18 that some signs will accompany true disciples and confirm that the gospel message is genuine. *And these signs will accompany those who believe: In my name they will drive out demons; they*

REFLECTION
How do you minister to others? Are any of the signs of Mark 16:17-18 happening in your life?

will speak in new tongues; they will pick up snakes with their hands; and when they drink deadly poison, it will not hurt them at all; they will place their hands on sick people, and they will get well.

This scripture speaks of various kinds of ministry to which the Lord calls His people today. It does not say that these signs shall follow pastors or apostles or evangelists. It says "these signs will accompany those who believe." Every Christian who truly believes in Jesus is called of God to be a minister to others and bring in the kingdom of God with power and authority.

Are we exercising spiritually?

In today's church, we often have a warped understanding of what it means to minister. But God is beginning to train and teach us to have a proper understanding of ministry from His perspective.

In the past, we have often thought that the pastor of the local church is responsible for all of the ministry—that the ministry is accomplished only by the clergy, the trained or the supported. Because of this attitude, many believers in the church today are very weak, understandably so. If you and I were to never exercise, we would become physically weak. In the same way, if we do not exercise spiritually, we become weak spiritually. *But solid food is for the mature, who by constant use have trained themselves to distinguish good from evil (Hebrews 5:14).*

We become spiritually mature by practicing and experiencing what God has told us to do. God has called every saint to be a minister for Him. We can be only a few days old in the Lord and already begin to minister to others by telling them what Jesus Christ has done for us.

When the pastor does all of the spiritual exercise, he burns himself out. The saints in the church are not exercising spiritually and remain weak, causing the entire church to be weak. Imagine a pastor doing four thousand push-ups every day! In a spiritual sense, that is what has happened in the church today.

I firmly believe that the Lord has called pastors and other spiritual leaders to train the saints so that every believer can be involved in ministry and maturing in Christ. When God's people are not exercising, they are no longer growing. Since God has given each of us different gifts and abilities, we all need to use these gifts to minister.

REFLECTION
How do we exercise our senses to discern good from evil (Hebrews 5:14)? What is lacking in a church where the pastor does all the ministry?

As each believer is fulfilling what the Lord has called him to do, a wonderful thing happens. God begins to build His church through His people from house to house and in each community. Ministry does not just happen in our church services; it happens at our schools, our places of work, and in our homes as we reach out to others. All, then, are fulfilled because they are using the gifts God has given them. This is the Lord's plan for building His church.

How to minister

There are various ways to minister. For example, washing someone's car or giving them a ride to work is a type of ministry. Others may be gifted to bake a cake, giving it to someone as a "labor of love." Encouraging others, praying for the sick, and serving children in a children's ministry or Sunday school are all types of ministry. Many times, people think that *to minister* means *to teach or preach*. But that is only one of hundreds of ways we can minister in the name of Jesus.

When Jesus walked on the earth, He could be at only one place at one time. God the Father's strategy was for Jesus to go to the cross, then be raised from the dead, ascend into heaven and later send the Holy Spirit to His people. The Holy Spirit then would indwell the Lord's people. Now, rather than only Jesus walking the earth offering hope to people, there would be thousands of believers filled with the same Holy Spirit, ministering in Jesus' name throughout the world.

We have received the Holy Spirit and are called by the Lord to be ministers. Everywhere Jesus went, He ministered to people. Everywhere we go, God has called us to minister to others—in our homes, communities, schools and jobs, and we can do it only by His strength. *Not that we are competent in ourselves to claim anything for ourselves, but our competence comes from God. He has made us competent as ministers of a new covenant—not of the letter but of the Spirit; for the letter kills, but the Spirit gives life (2 Corinthians 3:5-6).*

I will never forget the first time I ever taught at a Bible study as a young man. I was scared, because this was something new for me. I also realized that God's strength in me would pull me through. My competence was from God.

Many years ago, I served as a worship leader. The first time I ever led God's people in worship was in a church meeting where there were no musical instruments. I was given a small, round pitch pipe to get the proper key for the song. The first time, I blew the pitch pipe exceptionally loud and was extremely embarrassed! I looked for a hole in the floor to fall through, especially when I noticed that some of the people were giggling at my expense. It was a humbling experience, but by the grace of God I got through that first song. As I continued to practice, realizing I was called by God to minister in this way, I began to enjoy leading others in worshiping our Lord.

REFLECTION
List several things you are able to do for others. Where does your strength and ability come from according to 2 Corinthians 3:5-6?

DAY 5

Let's move out of our comfort zone

Each of us has an area in our lives that is comfortable, that we sometimes call our "comfort zone." We often find it hard to move out of our comfort zone into new things, but God has called us to take steps of faith. When Peter walked on the water, he moved far beyond his comfort zone!

God has called us to be people of faith and depend on the ability of God within us to help us accomplish His work. The Bible says, *...without faith it is impossible to please God (Hebrews 11:6).* Ministry to others will often require us to move beyond our comfort zone.

Our homes are excellent places of ministry. Jesus spent much of His time in the homes of people. The book of Acts is filled with examples of people meeting in homes: fellowshipping together, learning together and ministering to one another. Invite people into your home—for a meal or to spend time in fellowship. Exciting things can happen when people sit down together to eat a meal, play a game or just talk and laugh together. People can relax when we meet them on their own level and let them know we, too, are real people with real problems. We can ask the Lord for an opportunity to pray with them, and it can be a life-changing experience. Keep in mind that you are a saint who is called to minister.

The Lord may want to use you to give someone godly counsel. You may feel that since you're not a professional counselor, God can't use you, but the Bible says in Isaiah 9:6...*He will be called...Wonderful Counselor.* Jesus is the "Counselor" and He lives within us. When people need solutions to problems in their lives, and I don't know the answers, I know that Jesus, the Counselor, lives in me. He has the answers. I pray and ask the Lord to speak to them and tell them what to do. Sometimes I can steer them toward other Christians who may be able to answer their questions.

Remember, the Lord has given you a powerful testimony! As you share your testimony with others, you'll find that the Holy Spirit will use you to speak the truth and others will be built up in faith. Perhaps you are afraid someone will ask you a question that you don't have the answer to. If you are unsure of the correct answers, it is appropriate to say, "I don't

REFLECTION
Describe some situations when you moved out of your "comfort zone."

know, but perhaps I can ask someone who does know." None of us have all of the answers. That's why the Lord placed different gifts in different people in His church. We need one another.

It is not our ability, but His

The Lord wants us to be available for Him to use us to minister to others in many different ways. When our new cell-based church first started, one Sunday morning I was responsible to preach and the next Sunday morning I was responsible to minister to the children. Ministering to the children helped prepare me for other types of ministry the Lord would call me to in future years.

Regardless of the ministry the Lord has called you to, you do not minister by your own ability but by His ability that is within you. If you serve in a nursery, you can pray, laying your hands on these special children, ministering to them in Jesus' name. God has called each of us as Christians to minister wherever we go, asking the Lord to open our eyes so we can see people as He sees them. John 3:16 tells us, "God so loved the world that He gave His only begotten Son, that whoever believes in Him should not perish but have everlasting life." God loves people, and He lives in us! He has called us to encourage and serve the people around us.

Service is often done in practical ways. The Lord may call you to minister by helping a neighbor change a flat tire in the rain. God will be repairing a car through you! Sometimes serving requires us to do what the Lord has called us to do rather than what we *feel* like doing. If we have been truly crucified with Christ, the Bible tells us we are dead to doing what we want to do. *I have been crucified with Christ and I no longer live, but Christ lives in me. The life I live in the body, I live by faith in the Son of God, who loved me and gave himself for me (Galatians 2:20).*

The old "you" is dead and Jesus Christ now lives inside of you. He has called you to be a minister for Him.

Love conquers all

I was speaking to a professional counselor who had years of psychological training. "You know," he said, "some people think that in order to help others they need to have all kinds of training." Then he went on to say, "I find that what people really need is just to have someone to love them." This counselor was not minimizing the need for training; however, he was talking about meeting the deeper need that is in the hearts of men and women today—the need to be loved.

That is what ministry is really all about. Jesus has called us to love people. We love people by listening to them and genuinely caring about the needs they have. We should not feel fearful or inadequate to minister to others. The Bible says...*perfect love drives out fear...(1 John 4:18).*

When I realize that God loves me and He loves the person to whom I am ministering, His perfect love will cast out the fear. The more we spend time with Jesus, the more Christ will be able to minister through us. As we spend time with Jesus, those around us will perceive that we have the ability to minister to them because His love and boldness will be evident in our lives just as it was with Peter and John. *When they saw the courage of Peter and John and realized that they were unschooled, ordinary men, they were astonished and they took note that these men had been with Jesus (Acts 4:13).*

When we feel weak, it is then that we can be truly strong, because we know God's grace is sufficient for us. Paul pleaded with the Lord to take away a "thorn in the flesh." But the Lord told him that His strength would be made perfect through Paul's weakness, according to 2 Corinthians 12:9-10. *But he said to me, "My grace is sufficient for you, for my power is made perfect in weakness." Therefore I will boast all the more gladly about my weaknesses, so that Christ's power may rest on me. That is why, for Christ's sake, I delight in weaknesses, in insults, in hardships, in persecutions, in difficulties. For when I am weak, then I am strong.*

God's grace is always sufficient to live our daily lives. When we draw near to Christ, He will help us in every situation, giving us strength and comfort. We can minister to others by faith, through the strength of Jesus Christ.

REFLECTION
What does perfect love do (1 John 4:18)? How does the grace of God operate in your life?

CHAPTER 2

We Are Called to Serve

KEY MEMORY VERSE

...whoever wants to become great among you must
be your servant, and whoever wants to be first must
be your slave—just as the Son of Man did not
come to be served, but to serve,
and to give his life as a ransom for many.
Matthew 20:26-28

What to do, if you want to be great

One day the mother of James and John came to Jesus with a special request. *Then the mother of Zebedee's sons came to Jesus with her sons and, kneeling down, asked a favor of him... "Grant that one of these two sons of mine may sit at your right and the other at your left in your kingdom" (Matthew 20:20-21).*

The Bible tells us that the other disciples were indignant. They couldn't believe that James and John had the audacity to expect to sit on the right and left hand of Jesus in His kingdom. They, of course, were still thinking that Jesus was going to set up an earthly kingdom here on earth. The twelve disciples had a wrong understanding of ministry and leadership entirely. Jesus tried to correct this wrong thinking when He told His disciples...*You know that the rulers of the Gentiles lord it over them, and their high officials exercise authority over them. Not so with you. Instead, whoever wants to become great among you must be your servant, and whoever wants to be first must be your slave—just as the Son of Man did not come to be served, but to serve, and to give his life as a ransom for many (Matthew 20:25-28).*

Jesus told His disciples that those who are under the world's system do not understand the principle of ministry and servanthood. Someone who is a leader in the world is often a person who exercises his power and control over people. But Jesus advocated a new way. He said that true leadership exemplifies servanthood. Servanthood is characterized through serving. Jesus Christ, the king of the universe, came to this earth to be a servant. Every chance He got, He served people and set an example for us. We also are called to be ministers (servants) to others in His name. We must minister to and help others—this is a true measure of greatness.

REFLECTION
What should you do if you want to be great, according to Matthew 20:26?
What did Jesus say that He came to do on the earth in Matthew 20:28?

Serving and ministry—one and the same

What, then, does it really mean to serve? As was mentioned earlier, the word *serving* and *ministry* are really synonymous. James and John wanted to be great in the kingdom. They thought greatness came from having the right position, but Jesus said greatness came through serving. Greatness does not depend on our talents or our abilities, but on our willingness to serve.

A servant is simply a person who is devoted to another. I love to watch people. And as I travel throughout the world, I've found an amazing truth. Wherever I find a truly "great man or woman of God," I notice that he or she has the heart of a servant.

Years ago, as a young pastor, I was at a leadership meeting in Dayton, Ohio. I found myself watching an elderly man, a leader in the body of Christ, who has now gone on to be with the Lord. Everywhere he went, he served others. I watched him as he reached out to a bell boy in the hotel, telling him about Jesus Christ. I watched him as he responded in gentleness and compassion to those who came and asked him questions about spiritual things. He was truly a servant.

The mark of greatness in the kingdom of God is our willingness and obedience to serve others. One day, Jesus told a parable to a group of guests who were invited into the house of a ruler of the Pharisees. *When someone invites you to a wedding feast, do not take the place of honor, for a person more distinguished than you may have been invited. If so, the host who invited both of you will come and say to you, "Give this man your seat." Then, humiliated, you will have to take the least important place. But when you are invited, take the lowest place, so that when your host comes, he will say to you, "Friend, move up to a better place." Then you will be honored in the presence of all your fellow guests. For everyone who exalts himself will be humbled, and he who humbles himself will be exalted* (Luke 14:8-11).

The Lord warns us that we should never exalt ourselves or try to take the best places. Instead, we need to be willing to serve in the background. D. L. Moody, the great evangelist of the last century who was used of God to see more than one-million souls come into God's kingdom, always liked to sit in the background. He was truly a servant. If we honor the Lord with humility and servanthood, in due time we will be exalted.

REFLECTION

In what ways are servant-leaders exalted by the Lord? Describe ways you have served in the background.

Serving in love

A friend of mine serves as a Christian leader in our nation. Years ago, when he was a young Christian, he moved to a major city. He has a charismatic personality and had studied the Bible. He was enthusiastic and excited to teach others. One evening he went to a Bible study and offered to teach the Word at future meetings. The group leader told him he appreciated my friend's willingness; however, he really needed someone to set up the chairs. So week after week, my friend could be found setting up the chairs for the meeting. He was willing to be a servant, and today he is a noted leader in the body of Christ, teaching the Bible throughout the world.

The scriptures tell us in 1 Corinthians 8:1...*knowledge puffs up, but love builds up.* Too much knowledge can make us arrogant, but love will always build others up. I have met people who thought that to be involved in ministry meant they were called to preach or teach rather than serve the people of God. Preaching and teaching are valid ministries that are needed in the church today. However, all ministry, including the ministry of preaching and teaching, must come from a heart of love and compassion. Preachers and teachers who are called by God have a desire to serve those whom they teach. Only love will build people up. Too much knowledge, including knowledge of the Bible, without a heart of love and compassion, can cause us to be puffed up with pride.

Many times God's people need to minister in menial and practical ways before the Lord will release them into a ministry of preaching and teaching. Those who are willing to serve in these humble beginnings often are being prepared by the Lord to minister in greater ways because they have developed a servant's heart. Regardless of how much training or knowledge a person may have, the Lord is looking for those who are willing to serve. If we are willing to serve, He can truly make us great. If we are not willing to serve, regardless of our training or background, we cannot be great in the kingdom.

REFLECTION
What builds people up in the Lord, according to 1 Corinthians 8:1? How have you developed a servant's heart?

How can I serve you?

Why didn't Jesus take you and me to heaven as soon as we were born again? I believe the answer is so we can serve here on the earth and help many people come into His kingdom through a relationship with Jesus Christ. Consequently, the bottom line is this: Every believer is called to serve. We are called to serve our families, people at our place of employment, the people to whom we are committed in our small groups, and other believers in our local church. The question we should ask ourselves wherever we go is, "How can I serve today?"

Maybe in your church you could serve by participating in a drama ministry, or serve through clowning as you minister to children. You may be called to minister to prisoners. Some may serve by picking up litter in a neighborhood. Perhaps you could visit the elderly and pray for them or serve meals to those going through a stressful time in their lives. Providing transportation for someone in a time of need can be a tremendous act of service.

You are a true minister when you serve others. Jesus never said, "I am the king, come worship me." He simply served. James 4:10 says, *Humble yourselves before the Lord, and he will lift you up.*

Some time back, a pastor who had served the Lord faithfully for many years became a member of our church. One of the first questions that he asked when he came was, "How can I serve?" He was not thinking, "When can I preach a sermon?" He understood the importance of true ministry, serving in the body of Christ. It is people with the attitude of a servant whom the Lord will use to build His church in a powerful way.

I have found I am drawn to others who are willing to serve. As Jesus went about serving others, people were attracted to Him. When we have the heart of a servant, the Lord will cause people to be drawn to us so we can pray for them and minister to them. As we reach out beyond ourselves to serve others, people will be drawn into the kingdom of God. People usually do not come to Jesus because we have a lot of Bible knowledge, even though it is important to understand the scriptures. People are attracted to Christ when they see the heart of a servant exemplified through our lives.

REFLECTION
List some specific ways you have served others. How can you remain humble if you are recognized as an expert or authority on a subject?

Touching others by serving

According to the Bible, people around us will glorify our God in heaven because of the way they see us serve. Jesus said...*let your light shine before men, that they may see your good deeds and praise your Father in heaven (Matthew 5:16)*.

A family I know made a commitment one winter to keep two elderly neighbors' sidewalks clean after it snowed. They shoveled cheerfully, even though they got an extraordinary amount of snow that winter!

I served as a pastor for many years. Because of the many people who came to our church, I was not able to meet everyone who came to our Sunday services. There were simply too many people. But do you know who they met? They met the people who parked the cars, those who greeted them at the door, those who ushered them to their seats, those who invited them to a meeting in their small group and those who served their children in the children's ministry. They experienced Jesus in these precious saints who were ministering to them and their children. By this, they were drawn into the kingdom of God.

You see, it is Jesus working through each of us that makes all the difference in the world. As the people in our church touched those

REFLECTION
How do you let your light shine so people see Jesus?

around them with the love of Jesus Christ, hundreds of precious people became part of God's kingdom and became committed to our local church. Jesus used hundreds of ministers, through practical service, to minister to those whom God drew into His kingdom.

Everywhere I go, I find people in the church who have servants' hearts. One time in Africa, I was blessed by a businessman who was constantly finding opportunities to serve. He was not looking for a position in the church, but his desire was to be supported by his business so he could better serve Jesus and the people of God in his local church. He was truly a minister.

Although the Lord does call specific people to be supported by the local church so they can equip others to minister, let us never forget that *every* saint is called to be a minister.

The ministry of "helps"

Jesus spent His time training, encouraging and modeling for His twelve disciples what the kingdom of God was all about. These disciples also served Jesus in a ministry of *helps* similar to what we see in 1 Corinthians 12:28...*God has appointed these in the church: first apostles, second prophets, third teachers, after that miracles, then gifts of healing, **helps**, administrations, varieties of tongues (NKJ).*

The ministry of *helps* is a ministry of giving aid, assistance, support or relief to another person involved in ministry. It is giving practical assistance to someone so he can fulfill his responsibilities to God. Jesus' disciples helped Him fulfill the ministry that His Father had given to Him. A group of women also aided Jesus in His ministry (Luke 8:1-3) who served in many ways so that Jesus had time to pray, preach and minister healing to the people around Him.

One day, Jesus sent His disciples into Jerusalem to find a colt, untie it and bring it back to Him so He could ride it to Jerusalem (Matthew 21:1-11). Another time, the disciples prepared the upper room for the Last Supper (Matthew 26:17-30). They were serving in the ministry of helps.

Yet another time, thousands of people were gathered together to hear Jesus teach. It was getting late and the people were hungry. When Jesus asked what was available to eat, they discovered they had only five loaves of bread and two fish. Jesus prayed over the loaves and fish, it supernaturally multiplied—in fact, twelve basketfuls were left over after all the people were fed (Matthew 14:13-21). The disciples were involved in the ministry of helps as they distributed the food to the hungry people. I personally believe there was one leftover basketful of food for each disciple who had served.

Another time, Jesus realized He needed to pay the temple tax, so He sent Peter to catch a fish. When the fish was caught, a coin was found to pay the taxes! (Matthew 17:27). Peter was serving in the ministry of helps when he caught the fish and paid the taxes.

REFLECTION
What is the ministry of helps? Have you ever served in this kind of ministry? How?

I am constantly looking for future spiritual leaders. The leaders God is looking for are those who are willing to serve in the ministry of helps as God prepares them for future leadership.

Training for future ministry

Jesus' disciples learned faithfulness by serving practically. If we are faithful in small things, God knows He can trust us with greater responsibilities. *He who is faithful in what is least is faithful also in much; and he who is unjust in what is least is unjust also in much (Luke 16:10 NKJ).*

Moses was trained to be a leader by serving. Before he delivered the children of Israel out of Egypt, God placed him in the ministry of helps—serving his father-in-law by tending sheep in the desert for forty years.

Later on, Joshua served Moses in a ministry of helps capacity while he was being trained to take over Moses' responsibility of leadership for the children of Israel. Many men and women of God today have been trained through practically serving another Christian leader for years before the Lord opens up a door of public ministry or leadership for them.

In fact, Jesus Himself spent thirty years in His father's carpentry shop—in the ministry of helps. Stephen and Philip were powerful evangelists; however, they both were also involved in serving tables (Acts 6:1-7). I encourage you to ask yourself, "How can I serve a leader whom the Lord has placed in my life?" Tell him or her you are willing to serve in the ministry of helps as the Lord trains you for future ministry.

For years, I served in the ministry of helps in a youth outreach. We played basketball and other sports with young people so we could share Christ with them. My responsibility in the basket-

REFLECTION

If we serve in small things, what happens, according to Luke 16:10?

ball club was to bring the basketball and to be the chauffeur who brought the young people to the basketball court week after week. Sometime later, I was asked to take a small group of new believers and start a believers' Bible study. The Lord used these acts of serving in my life to train me for future ministry.

If you want to find your ministry, a place to start is by serving in the ministry of helps as prescribed in the Word of God. Often, those people who try to push themselves into the limelight are the very ones who need to serve behind the scenes where the Lord can work His heart of a servant in them. I believe God desires to exalt us, but He asks us to humble ourselves first, so He can exalt us in due time (1 Peter 5:6).

CHAPTER 3

Ministering with Compassion

Loving regardless of the response

Whenever Jesus ministered to others, His ministry came from a heart of love and compassion. *When he saw the crowds, he had compassion on them, because they were harassed and helpless, like sheep without a shepherd (Matthew 9:36).*

Jesus loved the people He served and has called us to do the same. 1 Corinthians 13 is often known as the "love chapter" in the Bible. The scriptures in this chapter teach us that we can do all kinds of good deeds and "ministry," but unless it is done from a heart of love, it will be of no profit for us or others.

Love is not just a feeling but a decision you make. *Love is giving with no expectancy of return.* Jesus Christ loved us. He went to the cross and made a decision to love us regardless of our response to Him. In the same way Jesus gave His life for us, He has called us to love others and give our lives for them. We can love others because Jesus Christ loved us first. Since Christ lives in us, His love is in us. Every day we need to allow the love of God to be released in our lives. Either we live by what the Word of God says and by the truth of Christ living in us, or we live by our emotions and by the way we feel. Here is an excellent checklist to use as you minister to others: *But the wisdom that comes from heaven is first of all pure; then peace-loving, considerate, submissive, full of mercy and good fruit, impartial and sincere (James 3:17).* If you want to give someone counsel, you can readily decide whether or not you have Christ's compassion by asking: "Am I willing to yield?" "Is the counsel I'm giving pure?" "Is it bringing peace, or is it bringing confusion?" God is not the author of confusion but of peace (1 Corinthians 14:33 NKJ).

REFLECTION
What is the difference between serving with compassion and serving without compassion? Name the things on the checklist of James 3:17 that will be evident as you minister to others.

Many times we may say the right thing but in a wrong attitude. This will not produce the spiritual results that God desires. We can respond like a lamb or a snake to those around us. A lamb is willing to yield and even be taken to the slaughter (Isaiah 53:7). The devil will always rise up in resistance like a snake: "Who are *you* telling *me* what to do?" God has called us to respond to others and minister to them like a lamb—with love and compassion.

Start small

As we minister to others out of a heart of love and compassion, we need to recognize that there are many different kinds of ministries the Lord has given to His people. 1 Corinthians 12:4-7,11 says, *Now there are diversities of gifts, but the same Spirit. There are differences of ministries, but the same Lord. And there are diversities of activities, but it is the same God who works all in all. But the manifestation of the Spirit is given to each one for the profit of all: But one and the same Spirit works all these things, distributing to each one individually as He wills (NKJ).*

I have met people who feel they are called to minister to others by singing or leading in worship when, in actuality, they cannot carry a tune. The Lord simply has not given them the ability to sing. We need more than an inward motivation for a spiritual gifting, we also need to be enabled to perform it. God is the One who gives us the power to perform ministry of any kind. We will know when we are functioning in the ministry God has given us because it will produce certain results.

A great place to begin to minister to others is in a small group setting such as a cell group or house church. Maybe God has called you to prophesy. Start in your small group. Perhaps the Lord has given you a song to sing that would be a blessing to other believers. The place to start is in a small group of believers. When you are faithful in this smaller setting, the Lord can then release you in larger settings in the future.

Sometimes people have what may be called a "preacher's itch." They constantly think they are responsible to preach and teach at every meeting they go to. Desiring to preach the Word is a very noble desire. However, ministry

REFLECTION
How can you begin to allow the Lord to use you in your spiritual gift(s)? Do others recognize the gift(s) in you?

is serving. As was mentioned in the last chapter, Stephen and Philip served tables, and then God released them as mighty evangelists. They started by practical service. We should follow their example.

What counts for eternity

Many years ago we spent much of our time ministering to a group of young people who grew up in homes without Christ. One day, some of these youngsters sat on our Volkswagen's sunroof, damaging it. From that time on, whenever it rained, water would leak from the roof and drip on my knee as I drove. For awhile, I had to watch my attitude. Was it really worth it to minister to these young rowdy people who caused my car's sunroof to leak and showed no appreciation for what we did for them? Soon I realized, "What does it matter anyway?" All that matters is where these youngsters spend eternity. Today, some of those young people are dynamic Christians.

As we see life from God's perspective, we realize that all that really counts is our relationship with God and our relationship with others as we serve those around us. God's call on our lives is first to love Him, and then to love people. Paul, the apostle, said in 1 Corinthians 9:22, *To the weak I became weak, to win the weak. I have become all things to all men so that by all possible means I might save some.*

If we really love people with the love of Jesus Christ and see them from God's perspective, we will be willing to do whatever it takes to relate to help them come to know Jesus and fulfill the call of God that is on their lives. Many issues that we consider of major importance are really minor in God's eyes. Let's just love Jesus and one another and realize we are ministers. Then let's reach out to those around us in His name. God is calling many kinds of people to become part of His church, according to Galatians 3:28. *There is neither Jew nor Greek, slave nor free, male nor female, for you are all one in Christ Jesus. If you belong to Christ, then you are Abraham's seed, and heirs according to the promise.*

I get excited when I go to a meeting of believers and see them loving and accepting one another. One person wearing a suit sits next to someone wearing an old pair of jeans. There are no social, national, racial or gender distinctions with regard to our relationship with the Lord. It is not what is on the outside that is so important, but what is on the inside—a heart that is being changed by Jesus Christ.

REFLECTION

How can you "become all things to all men" (1 Corinthians 9:22)? Why is it important to love all people, regardless of race, culture, gender, social position, wealth or age?

God uses imperfect people

Let's take a moment and look at the kind of people that God calls into leadership to minister effectively to others. This may surprise you. Let's start with Moses. *But Moses said to God, "Who am I, that I should go to Pharaoh and bring the Israelites out of Egypt?" And God said, "I will be with you..." (Exodus 3:11-12).*

Moses didn't feel like he was capable to do the job the Lord was asking him to do. Most Christians called to ministry feel the same way. They know they will have to rely on God's strength and not their own. The first small group Bible study I ever led seemed like a monumental task, but I took a step of faith because I knew God would give me the strength. Joshua was fearful when he responded to the Lord's call on his life. God told Joshua, *Have I not commanded you? Be strong and courageous. Do not be terrified; do not be discouraged, for the Lord your God will be with you wherever you go (Joshua 1:9).*

The Lord had to continually encourage Joshua in his new role as a leader. We do not depend on our ability but upon God's ability in us. If you feel you do not have all the natural gifts you need to be able to minister to others effectively, be encouraged. You have a lot of company. Moses and Joshua and many others throughout the scriptures felt the same way. But God used them anyway. The Bible tells us God has chosen to use imperfect people to fulfill His purposes to confound the wisdom of those who seem to be wise in this world (1 Corinthians 1:27).

REFLECTION
Describe any times you felt inadequate to minister but the Lord gave you the grace to do it. What does the Lord promise in Joshua 1:9?

Do not be afraid

Gideon was another individual who struggled when the Lord called him to areas of ministry and leadership. *"But sir," Gideon replied, "if the Lord is with us, why has all this happened to us? Where are all his wonders that our fathers told us about...But now the Lord has abandoned us and put us into the hand of Midian."*

The Lord turned to him and said, "Go in the strength you have and save Israel out of Midian's hand. Am I not sending you?"

"But Lord," Gideon asked, "how can I save Israel? My clan is the weakest in Manasseh, and I am the least in my family."

The Lord answered, "I will be with you, and you will strike down all the Midianites together" (Judges 6:13-16).

Have you ever felt like Gideon? You may know the Lord has called you to minister, and yet when you look at your own "track record," you can hardly believe it is possible that the Lord could use you. Yet if you seek to serve the Lord, He promises to be with you (Matthew 28:19-20).

Jeremiah was another individual who felt the same way that many young people feel when they realize God has called them to minister to others. Jeremiah, a young man, told the Lord in Jeremiah 1:6-8.

"Ah, Sovereign Lord," I said, "I do not know how to speak; I am only a child."

But the Lord said to me, "Do not say, 'I am only a child.' You must go to everyone I send you to and say whatever I command you. Do not be afraid of them, for I am with you and will rescue you," declares the Lord.

REFLECTION
Have you ever refused God? How? Has He given you a second chance?

A feeling of "I can't do it" is a common thread that runs through each of these individuals' responses when the Lord called them to ministry and leadership. This is the type of person the Lord will use—those who are completely dependent on Him. No matter what your task is in life, the Lord promises to be with you and help you.

Maybe you feel you've made too many mistakes and the Lord can never use you again. Look at Jonah. After running from God and being swallowed by a great fish, the Bible states, *Then the word of the Lord came to Jonah a second time (Jonah 3:1).*

God is always the God of a second chance. We need to put all of our trust in Him. We must be convinced that if God doesn't show up, it's all over. God has a "track record" of using those who feel like they cannot do the job. Remember, man looks at the outward appearance, but God looks at the heart (1 Samuel 16:7). When our heart is at the right place—in complete submission to Him—it is amazing what the Lord can do to prepare and equip us for the responsibilities that lie ahead.

Connected and protected

God's purpose in the earth today is to build His church (Matthew 16:18). His universal church is made up of multitudes of local churches in every part of the world. Their goal is to preach the gospel, bringing men and women into a saving relationship with Christ. Each and every local church should desire to motivate their members to reach out. The early church leaders in Antioch got together to fast and pray, and then sent out a dynamic missionary team. *In the church at Antioch there were prophets and teachers...While they were worshiping the Lord and fasting, the Holy Spirit said, "Set apart for me Barnabas and Saul for the work to which I have called them." So after they had fasted and prayed, they placed their hands on them and sent them off (Acts 13:1-3).*

Paul and Barnabas were not sent out on a lone mission, the church supported and encouraged this missionary team, and they reported back to the church telling all that had happened. *From Attalia they sailed back to Antioch, where they had been committed to the grace of God for the work they had now completed. On arriving there, they gathered the church together and reported all that God had done through them...(Acts 14:26-27).*

This shows the importance of being sent out to minister from our local church and reporting back to them what the Lord is doing through us. God's desire is to continue to build His church—the congregations of believers in your local community. Jesus told His disciples that the gates of hell will not prevail against the church of Jesus Christ (Matthew 16:18).

Sometimes, because of zeal or a lack of understanding of the scriptures, Christians get excited about ministering to others without being properly connected to the local church. I have met various people through the years who have not been properly connected to the body of Christ and have gone through many kinds of struggles that were unnecessary. As we minister to others, it is important to be properly connected and protected through the local church.

REFLECTION
How are you connected to and protected by the church? What can happen if you are not connected?

We are all kings and priests

Although we may find it hard to admit, at times we base our understanding of God on our preconceived ideas and our past experiences. Baptists grow up with a Baptist understanding of the scriptures, and the same can be said of Methodists, Lutherans, Charismatics and so forth. Depending on our church's denomination, we are convinced that our brand of theology is correct.

The truth is, we should be sure what we believe is based on the Word of God and not on a distorted traditional understanding. The Berean Christians refused to take everything that Paul preached at face value. They went home and studied the scriptures to be sure that the things Paul said were really true...*for they received the message with great eagerness and examined the Scriptures every day to see if what Paul said was true (Acts 17:11).*

Is it possible that certain traditions we consider to be completely scriptural are not based on the Bible at all? Could it be that the real reason we do certain things is because our spiritual parents and grandparents did them? I've heard the story of a young mother who always cut off the ends of a whole ham before baking it in the oven. When she was asked why she always followed this procedure, she said, "Because Grandma did it that way." Little did she know that grandma's roast pan was too small for the entire ham—that was the only motivation grandma had to cut off the ends!

Some traditions are good; however, we need to be sure that our ways of thinking are the same as God's. I believe a poor tradition (unbiblical, unscriptural) in the church has been the understanding that the pastor should do all the ministry, while the other saints simply come week after week to be fed. As we've learned from the scriptures in this book, every saint is called to be a minister, otherwise the church will never be built as the Lord intended.

Many Christians today have elevated pastors of a local church as holy men who stand between them and the Lord. The scriptures tell us He has made all of us kings and priests. *And has made us to be a kingdom and priests to serve his God and Father...(Revelation 1:6).*

REFLECTION

How are you responsible for what you believe?
How does Revelation 1:6 relate to this responsibility?

We all have direct access to the Lord through the shed blood of Jesus Christ. Praise God for pastors, elders, and spiritual leaders the Lord has placed in our lives, but we should not expect them to do all of the ministry. We are called by God to minister to others. Our spiritual leaders should encourage us, equip us, and train us to be servants who minister to others. Let's expect to be a minister today. Ask the Lord to open your eyes to see needs around you. Then expect the Lord to give you the grace and the strength to minister to others.

CHAPTER 4

We Are On Jesus' Team!

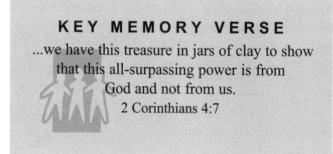

KEY MEMORY VERSE

...we have this treasure in jars of clay to show
that this all-surpassing power is from
God and not from us.
2 Corinthians 4:7

Live each day to the fullest

How would you feel if the President or Prime Minister of your nation personally asked you to serve on his team? I have even more awesome news for you—the King of the entire universe has hand-picked you as one of His personal ministers! When we get up in the morning, rather than dreading the day ahead of us, we can be assured that God wants to use us as one of His ministers. As we go to work, to school, or serve in our homes or communities, God has called us to be ministers. God is orchestrating His plans in our lives so we will meet people who need Jesus Christ and His ministry. As we trust Him in faith, He will unfold His plans before us.

One of the tricks of the enemy, aimed at trying to keep us from being fulfilled in God and in ministry, is to try to tempt us to live in the past. If that doesn't work, the enemy will tempt us to be overly concerned about our future. God wants us to live to the fullest in the present and allow Him to reign in the midst of our problems. Matthew 6:33-34 tells us, *But seek first his kingdom and his righteousness, and all these things will be given to you as well. Therefore do not worry about tomorrow, for tomorrow will worry about itself. Each day has enough trouble of its own.*

Every problem that you have is an opportunity for a miracle. As you read through the Bible, you'll find that every miracle was preceded by a problem. The Red Sea parted because the children of Israel had a problem—they had to flee the pursuing Egyptians. Jesus fed the five thousand because there was a problem—the people were hungry. The blind man was healed because he had a problem—he could not see. God desires to use you as an instrument of His miraculous power.

Sometime back, I was talking to a small group of people and I felt an impression from the Lord that one of the ladies was living with a fear that had been tormenting her for many years. As I shared this with her and the others in the room, she began to cry. We prayed for her, and Jesus ministered His peace and healing. Keep your eyes open, there are needs all around you. You can speak words that bring life to others.

REFLECTION
What are the things that will be given to you when you seek God's kingdom first (Matthew 6:33-34)?
When you speak words of encouragement to others, what happens?

Expect Jesus to use us

Some Christians believe they need to have their whole life planned out for them. But really, the way to live for Jesus is one day at a time. Life is much like a football game. The football coach could not possibly plan out every play, because every play is dependent on the plays the opposing team has just made. In the "game of life," the enemy has plans and God has plans. We stand in the middle of the playing field. Let's trust Jesus day by day and minute by minute and expect Him to use us to minister to others.

When we learn to fellowship with the Lord and listen to His voice, we will realize that He is always at work around us. Jesus said, *...My Father is always at his work to this very day, and I, too, am working...I tell you the truth, the Son can do nothing by himself; he can do only what he sees his Father doing, because whatever the Father does the Son also does. For the Father loves the Son and shows him all he does. Yes, to your amazement he will show him even greater things than these* (John 5:17,19-20).

What is God the Father doing around you right now? Let's find out what the Father is doing and then partner with Him as one of His vital ministers. Remember—God is the initiator; we are the re-sponders. *No one can come to me unless the Father who sent me draws him...(John 6:44).*

God is drawing people to Jesus Christ. Let's watch and pray and then respond as the Holy Spirit leads us to minister to others.

REFLECTION
How do we discover God's plan for our lives?
How do we partner with Jesus to minister to others?

Minister out of His love

Never forget—even though it is important to minister to others, God desires a personal love relationship with each of us. He really loves us. How can we know that Jesus loves us? Because He laid down His life for us at the cross 2000 years ago. Jesus loves us as much as the Father loves Him!

As the Father has loved me, so have I loved you. Now remain in my love. If you obey my commands, you will remain in my love, just as I have obeyed my Father's commands and remain in his love. Greater love has no one than this, that he lay down his life for his friends (John 15:9-10,13).

My daughter once prayed with a young lady in another nation. "Do you love Jesus?" she asked her. "Oh yes," the young lady responded, "but I do not love God the Father." She went on to explain that her father had molested her and, because of this devastating experience, she could not trust the Father in heaven. My daughter explained to her that God, our heavenly Father, loves her perfectly.

How do we know God loves us perfectly? Because of the cross. Jesus went to a cross and died for us. The cross of Jesus Christ is the proof of His love. As we minister to others, we need to minister out of an understanding that God loves us. We never should minister to *be* accepted by God or others. We minister because we *are* accepted by God, and we are able ministers of His love. In Isaiah 43:4, God expresses His love for Israel. *Since you are precious and honored in my sight, and because I love you....*

That same love applies to you and me today. God really loves you! He has redeemed us and we belong to Him. As we experience this love, we then can effectively minister that love to those around us. Lovers tell one another every day that they love each other. We need to tell our God how much we love Him. Jesus has told us in His Word over and over again how much He loves us. We can be effective in ministering to others as we experience our God's acceptance and love in our own lives.

REFLECTION
What have you learned about God's love from the above verses in the book of John? How can we love others like Jesus?

Partner with Jesus

DAY 4

We are privileged to partner together with God and be involved in what He is doing on the earth today. The Bible tells us in John 15:16, *You did not choose me, but I chose you and appointed you....*

God chose to use us. When I was a young boy, I played baseball with my school mates. However, since I was not a very good baseball player, sometimes I was not chosen for the team. I can remember standing in a row of young boys, waiting to be picked to play on the team. It felt so good when I was chosen. God wants you to know that He has chosen you to serve on His team. He has appointed you to bear fruit for Him.

Biblical Foundations

Everywhere you go this week, ask Jesus, "Lord, what are You doing around me? Open my spiritual eyes to see as You see. I know that You love me, so how do You want me to be involved in Your work this week?" Maybe He wants you to give an encouraging word to someone or write them a note.

Perhaps the Lord will lead you to pray for someone who needs to be encouraged and strengthened. The Lord may call you to minister to some children or listen to someone who has been going through a stressful time in their lives.

I don't know why God chose to use people, but He did. If I was God, I probably would not have chosen to use people. We make so many mistakes as human beings. But God chose to use us for His purposes on this planet. Let's remain secure in His love for us, so we can minister effectively to others in His name.

DAY 5

Decide to obey

In order to be effective as a believer in Jesus Christ, we need to make a decision every day to obey Him as His minister. Paul wrote to the Corinthian church encouraging them to obey the Lord in everything, no matter what came their way. *The reason I wrote you was to see if you would stand the test and be obedient in everything (2 Corinthians 2:9).*

Life is a series of decisions. Today you will make decisions that may affect the rest of your life. Let's be sure to constantly acknowledge the Lord in all of our decision-making, so we can truly partner together with Jesus to be His minister.

Naaman, in the Old Testament, desiring to be healed, came to the prophet Elisha (2 Kings 5). Elisha told him to wash in the Jordan River seven times. At first he reacted negatively, but then he made a decision, at the prompting of his servants, to obey the voice of the prophet. As he washed in the Jordan River, he was made whole. Obedience paid off for Naaman.

It always pays to be obedient. Every day you and I have the opportunity and privilege to be a minister to others. The enemy will try to cause us to be self-centered and think only of ourselves and our own needs and problems. However, when we make a decision in

Jesus' name each day to be a partner with Jesus, life takes on a whole new meaning.

I'm very grateful to those who have ministered to me. I'm grateful for the young lady who told me about Jesus Christ many years ago. I'm grateful for a pastor who was patient with me and ministered to me when I was baptized with the Holy Spirit. I'm grateful for my parents and others who provided for me when I was a young boy as they ministered to me in practical ways. I'm grateful for other believers who have encour-

REFLECTION
How do you obey Jesus in your decision-making?

aged me. The Bible tells us that much will be required of those who receive much (Luke 12:48). God has been very good to us. He now requires us to minister to others. Let's make a decision today to do it!

DAY 6

Please God rather than man

As you reach out in faith and minister to others, you will find there will be times you will be misunderstood. For example, when Jesus ministered healing to the blind man, both Jesus and the man who was healed were misunderstood. When the religious leaders asked the blind man if he thought Jesus was a sinner or not, he replied, ...*Whether he is a sinner or not, I don't know. One thing I do know. I was blind but now I see! (John 9:25).*

This man refused to defend himself. He simply spoke the truth. When you and I choose to obey the living God and minister to others in Jesus' name, we should not be surprised if there are times we are misunderstood. Remember—it is God whom we serve first, not man. We will find that everyone will not always understand. Jesus and His apostles were misunderstood many times. In fact, Paul, the apostle, writes, *Am I now trying to win the approval of men, or of God? Or am I trying to please men? If I were still trying to please men, I would not be a servant of Christ (Galatians 1:10).*

Pleasing God must be our top priority. If we desire to please people rather than please God, we are no longer effective as ministers of Jesus Christ. When I was baptized with the Holy Spirit, many people misunderstood—even well-meaning people. Some-times, when I have the privilege of leading people to faith in Jesus Christ, their friends and family members have been upset at me. But this is the price we may have to pay as believers in Jesus Christ who are called to minister to others.

When we minister to others in Jesus' name, we are called to love them and speak in a way that brings God's peace and blessing on them. *If it is possible, as far as it depends on you, live at peace with everyone (Romans 12:18).* However, we cannot focus on pleasing others more than pleasing Jesus. The early apostles declared boldly, "We ought to obey God rather than men" (Acts 5:29).

REFLECTION
Did you ever endeavor to live at peace with someone, but had to obey God first?

God has chosen you

One of the greatest ways for us to experience and continue to build a love relationship with the Lord is to partner with Him. He desires to do His greater works through us. *I tell you the truth, anyone who has faith in me will do what I have been doing. He will do even greater things than these, because I am going to the Father. And I will do whatever you ask in my name, so that the Son may bring glory to the Father. You may ask me for anything in my name, and I will do it (John 14:12-14).*

During the year that I was engaged to be married, we spent much of our time in ministry to young people. As we partnered together in ministry, the Lord allowed us to get to know one another better. This same concept is true in our relationship with our Lord Jesus. As we partner with Jesus and minister to others, we will continue to get to know Him more intimately.

Keep your "spiritual eyes" open. What is Jesus doing in your life, in the lives of your loved ones or in the lives of those He has placed around you? How has He called you to partner with Him to minister and serve others? Expect the Lord to use you today, and remember ... *we have this treasure in jars of clay to show that this all-surpassing power is from God and not from us (2 Corinthians 4:7).*

We have the treasure, our Lord Jesus Christ, within us. The power we have to minister to others is not of us—it is from Him. We are weak "jars of clay," but Jesus lives powerfully within our human weakness.

When you lay hands on sick people and pray, expect them to recover. Christ lives in you! As you speak words of encouragement to others, expect the Lord to use you to boost their faith. And never forget—God, the King of the whole universe, has chosen *you* as one of His choice ministers!

Everyone Can Minister

1. We are equipped to minister

a. Church leaders are in place to equip every believer to minister (Ephesians 4:11-12).

b. When leaders train believers to minister, they ease their burden and can "give themselves to prayer and ministry of the Word" (Acts 6:3b-4).

2. Everyone can serve

a. To ministers means to serve, to wait, to attend. Every Christian is called to serve others.

b. Mark 16:17-18 tells of some signs that accompany true disciples and confirm that the gospel message is genuine. These signs are meant to follow all Christians, not just leaders.

3. Are we exercising spiritually?

a. We become weak spiritually when we do not exercise spiritually (Hebrews 5:14).

b. We exercise spiritually by practicing and experiencing what God told us to do—minister.

4. How to minister

a. Washing someone's car, baking a cake, praying for the sick, serving children in a children's ministry, teaching—all ways we can minister.

b. We are competent ministers (2 Corinthians 3:5-6).

5. Let's move out of our comfort zone

   a. It's sometimes hard to move from our comfort zone to new things, but God has called us to depend on His ability and faith (Hebrews 11:6).

   b. Homes are excellent places for ministry. You may be called to give someone godly counsel (Isaiah 9:6).

6. It is not our ability, but His

   a. Ask the Lord to open your eyes to ways you can minister so you can love people as Jesus loves them (John 3:16).

   b. Service to others is practical: help repair a car, minister in a church nursery, etc.

   c. We may not always feel like doing it, but we are dead to doing what we want to selfishly do (Galatians 2:20).

7. Love conquers all

   a. We cannot be fearful or feel inadequate to minister. 1 John 4:18

   b. Peter and John ministered with boldness even though they were "unschooled, ordinary men" (Acts 4:13).

   c. God's grace is sufficient to live our daily lives. 2 Corinthians 12:9-10

We Are Called to Serve

1. What to do, if you want to be great

   a. The mother of James and John came to Jesus requesting that her sons sit at his right and left side in His kingdom. Matthew 20:20-21

   b. Jesus corrected this wrong thinking: the world's system does not understand ministry and leadership. Matthew 20:25-28

   c. Jesus said true leadership exemplifies servanthood.

2. Serving and ministry—one and the same

   a. Jesus said greatness comes through serving.

     Ex: An elderly leader in the body of Christ is seen ministering to everyone he came into contact with—the bell boy, etc.

   b. We should not exalt ourselves (Luke 14:8-11).

3. Serving in love

   a. Learn to serve first, even if you have the skills to lead.

     Ex: A gifted young man asks to teach the Word at a Bible Study. The wise leader gives him the job of setting up chairs for the meeting week after week. The young man's willingness to serve showed the leader he was ready for greater things.

   b. Too much knowledge without a heart of compassion and willingness to serve, causes us to be puffed up with pride. 1 Corinthians 8:1

4. How can I serve you?

a. Every believer is called to serve. Humble yourself and He will lift you up (James 4:10).

b. When we serve, others will be drawn to us. Serve in drama ministry, minister to prisoners, pick up litter in your neighborhood, visit the elderly: the opportunities are endless!

5. Touching others by serving

a. When people around us see us serving, they will glorify God. Matthew 5:16

b. Believers in the body of Christ with servants' hearts draw others into God's kingdom by their example.

6. The ministry of "helps"

a. The disciples served Jesus in a ministry of helps similar to what we see in 1 Corinthians 12:28.

b. "Ministry of helps" is a ministry of giving aid, assistance, support or relief to another person involved in ministry.

Ex: Examples of biblical ministry of helps

> *Luke 8:1-3; Matthew 21:1-11; 26:17-30; 14:13-21; 17:27*

c. The Lord is looking for leaders who are willing to serve in the ministry of helps to prepare them for future leadership.

7. Training for future ministry

a. If we are faithful in small things, God can trust us with greater responsibilities (Luke 16:10).

Ex: Joshua served Moses, Moses served his father-in-law, Jesus spent his first 30 years in his father's carpentry shop, Stephen and Philip were powerful evangelists, but first they served tables (Acts 6:1-7).

b. Humble yourself by serving so God can exalt you. 1 Peter 5:6

Ministering With Compassion

1. Loving regardless of the response
    a. Jesus ministers out of love and compassion. Matthew 9:36

    b. Love is not just a feeling, but a decision.

    c. As we minister to others, use James 3:17 as a checklist.

2. Start small
    a. There are different kinds of ministries the Lord gives His people (1 Corinthians 12:4-7,11).

    b. Find a gift or talent the Lord has given you and start using it in a small group setting or in a family setting. The Lord will develop the ministry in you.

3. What counts for eternity
    a. If we truly love people, we will do what it takes to relate to them (1 Corinthians 9:22).

    b. We must love regardless of age, race, social status, etc. Galatians 3:28

4. God uses imperfect people
    a. Moses did not feel capable of the job God asked him to do. Exodus 3:11-12

    b. The Lord encouraged Joshua concerning His call on his life. Joshua 1:9

    c. Many do not feel adequate when God calls them, but we depend on God's ability, not our own. The Lord uses imperfect people to fulfill His purposes to confound the wisdom of the "wise" of this world (1 Corinthians 1:27).

5. Do not be afraid

a. Gideon and Jeremiah struggled when the Lord called them to leadership (Judges 6:13-16; Jeremiah 1:6-8)).

b. If you feel inadequate, the Lord promises to be with you. Matthew 28:19-20

c. If you feel you have made too many mistakes, God is a God of second chances (Jonah 3:1).

d. God looks at the heart of an individual (1 Samuel 16:7).

6. Connected and protected

a. Paul and Barnabas were not sent out alone, the church supported and encouraged them (Acts 14:26-27).

b. The Lord wants to build His church through us as we connect to our local church and reach out to minister.

7. We are all kings and priests

a. We should make sure what we believe is based on the Word of God (Acts 17:11).

Ex: Sometimes traditions are distorted. A young mother always cut off the ends of the ham before cooking it. She was following her grandma's example, but she discovered later her grandma did it because her roast pan was too small!

b. Sometimes traditions in the church are distorted. For example, the idea that a pastor should do all the work of ministry.

c. We are all capable to minister to others. We are kings and priests (Revelation 1:6).

We Are On Jesus' Team!

1. Live each day to the fullest
    a. We should not live in the past or worry about the future. Matthew 6:33-34

    b. Every problem is an opportunity for a miracle. Speak words of encouragement to others and minister to their needs.

2. Expect Jesus to use us
    a. Trust Jesus minute by minute, learn to fellowship with Him. He is always at work around us (John 5:17,19-20).

    b. Discover what the Lord is doing and partner with Him as one of His vital ministers.

    c. God is drawing people to Christ (John 6:44), and in response we can minister to them.

3. Minister out of His love
    a. The Lord wants a personal love relationship with us. He loves us so much (John 15:9-10,13; Isaiah 43:4).

    b. We minister because we have been accepted by God and we are able ministers of His love.

4. Partner with Jesus
    a. The Lord chose to use us to accomplish what He wants here on earth (John 15:16).

    b. Ask the Lord how He wants to use you—how you can partner with Him to minister to others.

5. Decide to obey

a. Paul encouraged believers to obey the Lord no matter what came their way (2 Corinthians 2:9).

b. Let's obey the Lord in ministering to others, instead of selfishly leading our own lives.

6. Please God rather than man

a. Sometimes when you minister to others, you will be misunderstand, just a Jesus and the man he healed were misunderstood (John 9:25).

b. Paul said he looked only for God's approval (Galatians 1:10). Pleasing God is our top priority.

c. When we minister, as much as possible, speak in a way that brings God's peace and blessing (Romans 12:18).

7. God has chosen you

a. The Lord wants to do His greater works through us.
John 14:12-14

b. Expect the Lord to use you. We are weak "jars of clay" but Jesus lives powerfully within our human weakness.
2 Corinthians 4:7

c. When you lay hands on the sick, expect them to recover, when you speak works of encouragement to others, expect the Lord to use you to boost their faith.

Chapter 1
Everyone Can Minister
Journaling space for reflection questions

DAY 1

What is the role of spiritual leaders in the church, according to Ephesians 4:11-12? How do these leaders train us to minister?

DAY 2

How do you minister to others? Are any of the signs of Mark 16:17-18 happening in your life?

DAY 3

How do we exercise our senses to discern good from evil (Hebrews 5:14)? What is lacking in a church where the pastor does all the ministry?

List several things you are able to do for others. Where does your strength and ability come from according to 2 Corinthians 3:5-6?

Describe some situations when you moved out of your "comfort zone."

What happened when you were "crucified with Christ"?
What things died and what things became new?
How can you minister in practical ways?

What does perfect love do (1 John 4:18)? How does the grace of God operate in your life?

Chapter 2
We Are Called to Serve
Journaling space for reflection questions

DAY 1

What should you do if you want to be great, according to Matthew 20:26? What did Jesus say that He came to do on the earth in Matthew 20:28?

DAY 2

In what ways are servant-leaders exalted by the Lord? Describe ways you have served in the background.

DAY 3

What builds people up in the Lord, according to 1 Corinthians 8:1? How have you developed a servant's heart?

List some specific ways you have served others. How can you remain humble if you are recognized as an expert or authority on a subject?

How do you let your light shine so people see Jesus?

What is the ministry of helps? Have you ever served in this kind of ministry? How?

If we serve in small things, what happens, according to Luke 16:10?

Chapter 3
Ministering with Compassion
Journaling space for reflection questions

What is the difference between serving with compassion and serving without compassion? Name the things on the checklist of James 3:17 that will be evident as you minister to others.

How can you begin to allow the Lord to use you in your spiritual gift(s)? Do others recognize the gift(s) in you?

How can you "become all things to all men" (1 Corinthians 9:22)? Why is it important to love all people, regardless of race, culture, gender, social position, wealth or age?

DAY 4   *Describe any times you felt inadequate to minister but the Lord gave you the grace to do it. What does the Lord promise in Joshua 1:9?*

DAY 5   *Have you ever refused God? How? Has He given you a second chance?*

DAY 6   *How are you connected to and protected by the church? What can happen if you are not connected?*

DAY 7   *How are you responsible for what you believe? How does Revelation 1:6 relate to this responsibility?*

Chapter 4
We Are On Jesus' Team!
Journaling space for reflection questions

DAY 1 *What are the things that will be given to you when you seek God's kingdom first (Matthew 6:33-34)? When you speak words of encouragement to others, what happens?*

DAY 2 *How do we discover God's plan for our lives? How do we partner with Jesus to minister to others?*

DAY 3 *What have you learned about God's love from the above verses in the book of John? How can we love others like Jesus?*

How does it feel to be a partner with Jesus?
How are you bearing fruit for Jesus?

How do you obey Jesus in your decision-making?

Did you ever endeavor to live at peace with someone, but had to obey God first?

What are the results of being a partner with the Lord (John 14:12-14)? Describe a time you felt weak, but the Lord gave you strength in your human weakness.

Daily Devotional Extra Days

If you are using this book as a daily devotional, you will notice there are 28 days in this study. Depending on the month, you may need the three extra days' studies given here.

DAY 29

What Has Changed?

Read John 5:1-9. How did Jesus respond to the man who had an infirmity for years? What can we learn from his example as we see people with needs around us? What Bible stories or verses from these lessons on ministry have had the biggest effect on your life? What further changes are you looking for?

DAY 30

Are You Called?

Read John 17:20-26. How is Jesus ministering to us through these verses? What does Jesus' example teach us regarding ministering to others? Do you have a sense of a strong calling from God to do a particular ministry? Would you be willing to start at the bottom? Explain.

DAY 31

Ministering to Others

Read John 19:25-27. How did Jesus' mother, Mary, and Mary Magdalene minister to Jesus in these verses?
How did Jesus minister to His mother in these verses?
How did John minister to Jesus' mother in these verses?
What can we learn from these examples?

Coordinates with this series!

Biblical Foundations for Children

Creative learning experiences for ages 4-12, patterned after the *Biblical Foundation Series*, with truths in each lesson. Takes kids on the first steps in their Christian walk by teaching them how to build solid foundations in their young lives. *by Jane Nicholas, 176 pages:* $17.95

Hearing God 30 Different Ways

Learn to "tune in" to God and discern "HIS" voice. God wants to speak to you. Includes a seminar manual.

Spiritual Fathering & Mothering Seminar

Practical preparation for believers who want to have and become spiritual parents. Includes a seminar manual.

Elder's Training Seminar

Based on New Testament leadership principles, this seminar equips leaders to provide protection, direction and correction in the local church. Includes a seminar manual.

Small Groups 101 Seminar

Basics for healthy cell ministry. Session topics cover the essentials for growing cell group ministry. Each attendee receives a *Helping You Build Manual.*

Small Groups 201 Seminar

Takes you beyond the basics and into an advanced strategy for cell ministry. Each attendee receives a seminar manual.

Counseling Basics

This seminar takes you through the basics of counseling, specifically in small group ministry and others. Includes a comprehensive manual.

Marriage Mentoring Training Seminar

Trains church leaders and mature believers to help prepare engaged couples for a strong marriage foundation by using the mentoring format of *Called Together.* Includes a *Called Together Manual.*

Seminars held at various locations throughout the US and Canada. For complete brochures and upcoming dates:

Call 1.800.848.5892
www.dcfi.org   email: info@dcfi.org